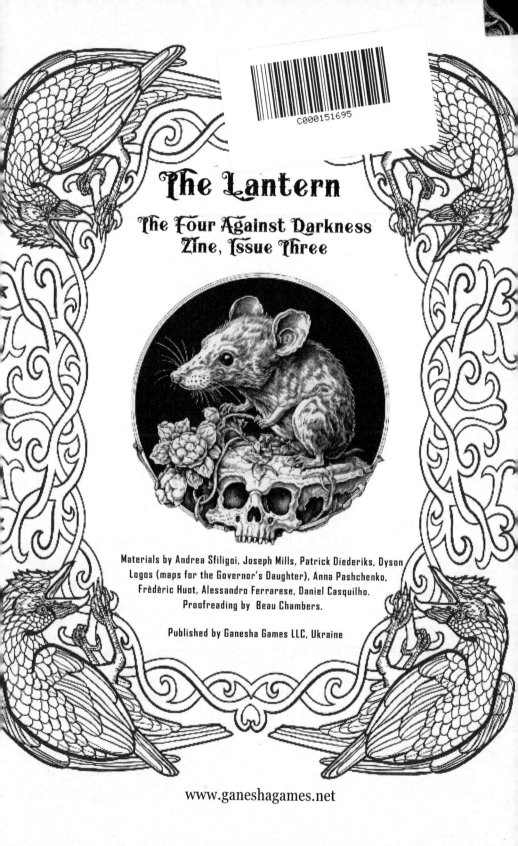

The Lantern

The Four Against Darkness Zine, Issue Three

Materials by Andrea Sfiligoi, Joseph Mills, Patrick Diederiks, Dyson
Logos (maps for the Governor's Daughter), Anna Pashchenko,
Frèdèric Huot, Alessandro Ferrarese, Daniel Casquilho.
Proofreading by Beau Chambers.

Published by Ganesha Games LLC, Ukraine

Table of Contents

Adventure: The Governor's Daughter, by Patrick Diederiks and Andrea Sfiligoi, maps by Dyson Logos   p.1

Adventure: The Halls of Thoral, by Alessandro Ferrarese and Andrea Sfiligoi, map by Alessandro Ferrarese   p. 9

Adventure: Quest for a Doll's Soul, by Frederic Huot and Andrea Sfiligoi   p. 26

4AD Houserule: Holy Symbols Expanded, by William C. Pfaff   p. 40

New Weird Monster:Zvuk, the Trumpeteer, by Anna Pashchenko   p. 42

Adventure: Setting up Camp, by Frédéric Huot   p. 45

Using Pre-Generated Maps, by Daniel Casquilho   p. 54

The Governor's Daughter

An adventure for L1–3 characters by Patrick Diederiks and Andrea Sfiligoi. Maps by Dyson Logos.

Alister, the youngest nephew of Murazzo, Captain of the Guild of Thieves, has done something foolish. He is madly in love with Esmeralda, the daughter of Lord Erid Orfeld – a former merchant of Dorantia and now its Governor, a very wealthy and powerful man, definitely not to be trifled with. Erid Orfeld is not fond of Alister, who is soft spoken. He will not allow a relationship between the two teenagers. So Alister made a desperate move. He ran away with Esmeralda. He wanted to hide in a shipwreck in Banana Bay, thinking she would be safe there.

What he didn't know was that the "Wight's Shadow" shipwreck is now inhabited by evil creatures led by an undead pirate king. The moment he brought Esmeralda aboard the shipwreck, skeletal pirates with tricorns and blunderbusses emerged from the shadows, captured her and threw him overboard, with a cackling laugh from their clinking jaws.

Once back in town, Alister overcame all his fears and went to the Governor to tell what had happened. He was ready to accept any consequence of his actions, if only the governor were willing to help free Esmeralda from the skeletal pirates.

The Wreck at
Banana Bay

After an outburst of anger, Lord Erid Orfeld reaches a decision. Alister will have to free Esmeralda and he will be accompanied by the party. Each surviving member of the party will be paid 50 gp upon delivery of the girl.

How to Play

To play this adventure you only need the *Four Against Darkness* core rules.

Entrance: You enter the shipwreck via storage room 17 or 18, your choice. Treat Alister as a 5th character. He is a L2 rogue, armed with a short sword (light slashing weapon) and wearing Light armor.

Rooms/Corridors: All smaller rooms are littered with wreckage and count as corridors.

Refer to *Four Against Darkness* for all rules (traps, Searching, treasure, Wandering Monsters, Secrets). Do not roll to determine which enemy is the final boss. Do not draw a map. Use the map on the next page. As you move to a numbered location, read its corresponding numbered paragraph. Do not read ahead. Roll a 1 in 6 chance of an encounter with Wandering Monsters when you move through a room you already visited. After completing your mission, you must exit the map.

Room Content table (d6)	
1	Treasure Room: Roll on the Shipwreck Treasure table
2	Empty. The area may be Searched.
3	Vermin encounter.
4	Minions encounter.
5	Empty. The area may be Searched, but on a d6 roll of 1, the character doing the searching falls through a rotten wood plank and loses 1 Life.
6	Boss Monster encounter.

Shipwreck Treasure table (d6)	
0 or less	No treasure found.
1	d6 gp or 1 length of rope or d3 food (choose).
2	2d6 gp.
3	Choose: you find either 1 pouch with 6+d6 gp or 1 pearl worth 3d6 gp. The roll for the value of the pearl uses the exploding die roll system, so if you are really lucky and roll a 6 on one or more dice, the pearl may be worth ANY amount.
4	Choose: 1 gem worth 2d6 x 5 gp, 1 light or hand weapon, or (if you have *Warlike Woes*) 1 herbal remedy of your choice (done with seaweed).
5	Choose: 1 item of jewelry worth 3d6 x 10 gp or 1 ranged weapon of your choice (bow, crossbow or sling).
6+	1 random magic item from the Magic Treasure table in 4AD.

THE WRECK OF THE WIGHT'S SHADOW

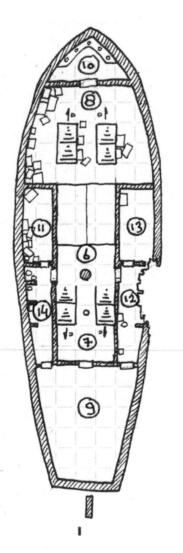
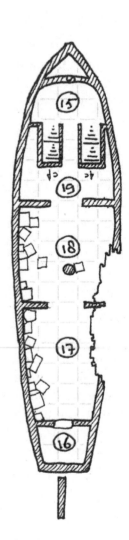

Maps by Dyson's Dodecahedron (Dyson Logos)

Guards

After visiting every 2nd tile, there is a 2 in 6 chance that d6 swashbuckler guards surprise you. A rogue may be able to hear the guards coming and prevent the surprise with a successful L4 hearing save. Add the rogue's L to the roll. Use the highest L rogue in the party. You get only ONE attempt to hear the guards. If the roll is successful, the party will act first. If the roll fails, the guards will surprise the party. Roll d6. On a 1-4, the guards' attack comes from the rear, and you must distribute attacks starting from characters in the last positions of the marching order. On a 5-6, it comes from the front and you must distribute attacks starting from characters in the front of the marching order.

Resolve the encounter for the guards after resolving any encounter in the room.

Wandering Monsters

When passing through a room you've already visited, roll a 1 in 6 chance of Wandering Monsters surprising your party.

Finding Esmeralda

After the first room, every time you enter a room occupied by Vermin, Minions or Bosses, roll a 1 in 6 chance that Esmeralda is held captive in that room. You must take her off board and into safety as soon as possible.

If you do not find her in any room, you will find her automatically in the last room of the ship wreck.

Concluding the Adventure

After his daughter is brought to him safely, Lord Erid Orfeld is filled with joy and gratitude. He may at this point be convinced to accept the relationship between the two teenagers.

If you want, you may roll a Persuasion save vs. L6. Add +1/2 L of your highest level character, or +L if the character is a rogue, and an additional +1 if the character is a cleric. On a success, Orfeld will bless the relationship and offer Alister a position as guard in his private guards regiment.

On a failure, Orfeld allows them to explore the world and have new adventures with the party. Alister and Esmeralda may each choose a weapon of their choice from the armory and both get an emerald with a value of 150 GP for unexpected cost which may may occur during their future travels. They may be played as rogues (Alister is L2, Esmeralda is L1) and you may equip them as desired and let them earn their own XP rolls.

If Alister dies, you can still rescue Esmeralda. If Esmeralda dies, the adventure fails and the party loses any faction points they could have with Orfeld – you will no longer be able to work for him. Orfeld becomes a sworn enemy of the party.

Adapting the Adventure for Higher Level Characters

To play this adventure with higher level characters, do the following:

1) Increase the L of all foes and Saves by the amount of Levels your average character is above L1; for example, if your party has an average of L5, increase by 4 all Levels and Saves.

2) Increase by d6 the number of Minor Foes (Minion/Vermin) per every Tier beyond the Basic. For example, add d6 Minion/Vermin at Expert Tier, add 2d6 at Heroic Tier, etc.

Encounters

Shipwreck Vermin table (d6)	
1-3	**4d6 Ship Rats**, L2 Animal Vermin, Morale -1, No Treasure. Any character wounded by the rats has a 1 in 6 chance of losing 1 additional Life due to an infected wound. Keep track of the number of times you encounter them. Every time you encounter them again, add +1 to their number for every rat encounter you had. *Reactions (1D6): 1–3 flee, 4–6 fight*
4-6	**2D6+2 Slippery Sea Worms**, L3 Animal Vermin, Normal morale, No Treasure. At the beginning of the encounter, there is a 2 in 6 chance that a random hero slips on the slippery monsters. The slipping hero will be unable to Attack on his/her first turn. *Reactions (1D6): 1 flee, 2 bribe (1 food), 3-4 fight, 5-6 fight to the death.*

Shipwreck Minions table(d6)

1-2	**d6+2 Skeleton Pirates**, L3 Undead minions, Crushing weapons attack at +1. Arrows attack them at -1. Immune to Sleep and Poison. Clerics add +L when attacking them. Skeleton Pirates never test for Morale. Their flashy pirate outfits are still in good condition and may be sold for 3 gp each. They are armed with cheap scimitars. If you pick these up, in the hands of your heroes they count as edged melee weapons that break on an Attack roll of 1. The cheap scimitars may also be sold for 4 gp each. They are also armed with blunderbusses that will perform 1 ranged attack each, at +1 (your characters must defend vs. a L4 ranged attack before the melee). *Reactions: Always fight to the death*
3-4	**d6+3 Sea Spawn**, L3 minions, normal Morale. No treasure. On an Attack roll of 1, the hero has touched the sea spawn and must save vs. L2 disease. On a failure, the hero develops "barnacle rot", and his hands become covered in barnacles, which gives a -1 modifier to all the hero's Attack rolls until a Blessing is used to counter the disease. *Reactions: Always fight.*
5	**d6+1 Guards**, L4 minions. Treasure +1, normal Morale. Guards have a 1 in 6 chance of surprising the party. A rogue with the party has a chance to perform a L4 hearing save to hear them coming and negate their surprise. If there are multiple rogues in the party, choose one to roll. Add ½ the rogue's L to the roll. *Reactions (1D6): 1-2 bribe (10 gp per guard), 3–5 fight, 6 fight to the death.*
6	**d3+1 Skeleton Guards**, L4 Undead minions. Crushing weapon attack them at +1. Arrows attack them at -1. Immune to Sleep and Poison. Clerics add +L when attacking them. They never test Morale. They are armed with short, cheap pikes. If used by the characters, these pikes count as two-handed slashing weapons and break on an Attack roll of 1. A broken pike may be used as a club (light crushing weapon). *Reactions: Always fight to the death.*

The Halls of Thoral

An adventure for a L1 Party for Four Against Darkness
Written by Alessandro Ferrarese

Background

You arrived a few weeks ago at the village of Ranth at the foot of the Peak of Mists. The mountain is famous for being the home of the ancient Thòral dwarves, a renowned clan of dragon slayers. Now the iron mines are under the rule of the burgomaster Elda Shavin. Once in the village, there are rumors of a rat infestation in the mines at the foot of the Peak of the Mists. Or maybe there is a curse on the mountain itself.

The burgomaster scolds villagers who gossip too much about this. She has to make sure that rumors of curses do not spread, as they aren't conducive to good business.

Your party is hired to investigate. There's no direct access to the mine. The only path available is through the halls of the dwarven manor, which has been uninhabited for centuries. After preparing for the journey, you set off for the Peak of Mist.

Introduction

The adventure is designed for a party of L1 characters. Events and encounters are already written in the story you are about to play. For everything else, the general rules of 4AD core rulebook apply. The adventure ends when the party returns to the initial village or if they are defeated.

Wandering Monsters

Whenever you return to a previously visited room or corridor (not necessarily to the paragraph!) roll 1d6. On a result of 1, a wandering monster will ambush your party. Roll on the Wandering Monsters of the Halls of Thòral Table at the end of the adventure to determine who does so.

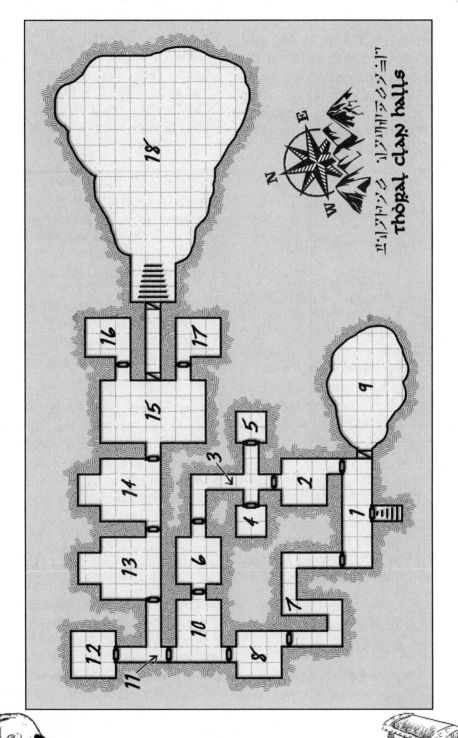

thopal clap halls

§1.

The entrance hall is damp and cold. On the opposite side, between two wooden pillars on each side, you see two doors: the one on the left seems closed, while the one on the right is open. The only noise you hear is the squeaking of small rats.

To Search the room, go to §19.

To go to the left, read §7.

To go to the right door, read §2.

§2.

This room was once a guardhouse. There are some worn out torches on the walls, and a small bed. A small rack still holds a couple of rusty axes and a wooden shield marked by a few blows. From the dimness at the back of the room, behind a small dark chest, small red eyes stare at you before launching themselves against you in search of 'food'.

You are attacked by 13 Rats.

Rats, L1 Animal Vermin, No Treasure. Characters wounded by the rats have a 1 in 6 chance of losing 1 additional Life due to infection at the end of the encounter).

If the party survives and you continue exploring, go to §3.

§3.

This corridor is empty. You may Search it with a -1 penalty to the roll. On a result of 0-1, roll on the Wandering Monsters of the Halls of Thoral Table to determine who attacks you. On a 2-4, the corridor is indeed empty. On a 5-6, you find 1 Clue. As soon as you find 3 Clues, read §32.

On either side of you there are two doors. In front of you the corridor continues to a bend that does not allow to see beyond, but from which you can hear hoarse voices speaking in an unknown language.

If you take the left door, read §24. To go through the right door, go to §5. To go deeper into the corridor until you reach the bend, read §27.

§4.

This probably used to be a small medical cabinet. On the few remaining shelves, you find a few dusty glass containers and a number of bandages, most of them unusable. You may spend some time looking for something useful here.

You may Search the room. On a result of 1, roll on the Wandering Monsters of the Halls of Thoral Table to determine who will attack you. On a 2-4, the room is indeed empty. On a 5-6, you find 1 bandage and 1 bottle containing a dry root. It's probably some healing herb. if at any moment you decide to consume it, read §28. If

you have an alchemist, conservationist or druid in the party, you may read §28 BEFORE consuming the root.

You may go back to §3 and choose a new path.

§5.

You enter a shabby old armory. Large stones fell from the walls and ceiling and now lie on the shattered floor. Many weapons and suits of leather armor are buried and unusable. In a corner of the room, however, you see a shining long sword and a shield still in good condition.

If you want to collect the sword and shield and there is an elf in the party, go to §33; otherwise, go to §21. You may also go back to §3 and choose another route.

§6.

The door is not completely closed, and you perceive that someone is inside.

To break down the door with magic (with a Fireball or Lightning spell/scroll) go to §29. To open it normally, go to §30.

§7.

This corridor is empty. You may Search it with a -1 penalty. On a 0-1, roll on the Wandering Monsters of the Halls of Thoral Table to determine who attacks you; on a 2-4, the corridor is indeed empty. On a 5-6, you find 1 Clue instead. When you find 3 Clues, go to §32.

At the end of the corridor, a new room opens up in front of you. Go to §8 to explore it.

§8.

The room was ransacked by someone. You find gnawed strips of dried meat and a few bits of moldy cheese. Moving some furniture and a few stones, you find the corpse of a greenish creature. Its long sharp teeth and long pointed ears leave no doubt, it's a goblin of the burrows. Its belly has been pierced by a blade and it is still covered in its own gore. While you look around for other details, you hear the sound of a plate shattering behind the door.

The room looks empty. You may Search it (go to §22) or continue to the next room (go to §10).

§9.

The walls become lower, forcing you to crawl along. Your effort is rewarded when you reach a large area carved out of natural stone. Numerous unlit braziers adorn the room. There is a decorated sar-cophagus of fine marble. You

approach it cautiously, but as you do so the corpse of a mummified dwarf stretches out its bony hands in your direction!

You are attacked by surprise by 1 Mummified Dwarf.

Mummified Dwarf, L5 Undead Boss Monster, 4 Life, 2 attacks, Treasure +2, Never tests Morale. Clerics attack it at +L . Any character killed by the mummified dwarf becomes a mummy and must be fought by the rest party. The Fireball spell and other fire-based attacks hit the mummified dwarf with a +2 bonus.

If you defeat the creature, you can retrace your steps, returning to §1 to choose another path.

Night Goblins, L3 Minions, Treasure -1, Never test Morale. Dwarves attack them at +1. At the start of each turn of the Night Goblins, roll 1d6. On a 1-5 nothing happens, on a 6 they grab and extinguish your lantern (you cannot relight it until you defeat them; heroes Attack and Defend at -2 in the darkness).

If you survive, you may take the goblin's loot and their cheap blades (they count as hand weapons or light hand weapons in your characters' hands, as you prefer; however, on an Attack roll of 1, they break and must be discarded).

You may now take the right door (go to §34) or the door in front of you (go to §11).

§10.

The room is large and spacious. On the left, there's a fireplace that once heated the room. Two large tables and several stools are overturned. You look for something useful, when some creatures emerge from the fireplace. You draw your weapons as you recognize their evil grin beneath the soot. Night goblins! They throw ash at you and draw their blades.
7 Night Goblins attack you.

§11.

The corridor continues a little further on to a new door, while on the right it turns and enters the darkness again. You move forward until you reach the junction. Here you see a party of orcs carrying heavy stones approaching.

You come across 3 Orcs:
Orcs, L4 Minions, Standard Treasure. Elves attack them at +1. Orcs are afraid of magic and must make a Morale roll every

time one of them is slain by a spell; if a spell causes their numbers to fall below half, roll at -1. They never have any magical items in their loot: should you get a scroll, consider it to be d6xd6 gp instead.

Reactions (d6): 1-2) Bribe (10 GP per monster), 3-5) Fight, 6) fight to the death).

If you defeat or bribe them you can continue to the door in front of you (go to §12) or go in the direction the orcs came from (go to §13).

§12.

Someone picked the lock that kept the door closed, using a crude method. In fact, a large part of the wood has been torn away, probably by an axe swing. Indeed, you see an open trapdoor. Apparently, an ogre fell into it and was impaled by the sharp stakes at its bottom. Walking cautiously around the trap, you enter the room. A pile of small gems lies on the floor. In the center of the room, there's a statue of a dwarf wielding a large hammer.

The room is empty. You may pick up the gems (worth 20 GP) and Search the room if you want. On a result of 1, roll on the Wandering Monsters of the Halls of Thoral Table to determine who attacks you. On a 2-4, the room is indeed empty. On a 5-6, you find 1 Clue. When you have found 3 Clues, go to §32.

Go back to §11 to choose another route.

§13.

In the room there are several picks and shovels, buckets and piles of stones scattered all around. The orcs you encountered were probably busy in this room and appear to have been digging vigorously in the northernmost wall. It is not clear why they were doing this. You turn to continue on your way, when suddenly from the burrow two trolls covered in dirt, emerge and rush you with shovels in hand.

2 Trolls attack you.

Trolls, L5 Minions, Standard Treasure. Halflings defend themselves at +L . Trolls regenerate, unless they are killed by a spell, or a character uses an attack to cut up their corpses. Roll 1d6 for each troll killed: on a 1-4, nothing happens. On a result of 5-6, the troll comes back to life and continue fighting during its next turn).

If you defeat them, you may continue to the next door (go to §35), or go back to §11 and choose another path.

§14.

The door crashes down. However, you are almost hit by a large projectile thrown in your direction. You see that it is a goblin thrown against the wall, its eyes bursting out of its sockets. The shooter is the largest ogre you have ever seen. His head is shaven clean and he is wearing a few layers of animal skins.

He was sitting on a stool, being massaged by a few frightened goblins. He stands up and grabs a large wooden beam with a rusty nail stuck through its end. The few goblins flee, unwilling to suffer the same fate as the corpse that is now slowly sliding down the wall beside you. The ogre stares at you defiantly, and in a hoarse voice speaks to you in the common tongue: "No destroy mission of my master!"

Fight the Ogre Boss.

Ogre Boss, L5 Boss Monster, 5 Life, 2 attacks, Treasure +1 (ignore magic items in his loot, if any: count them as 2d6xd6 gp instead), Never tests Morale. Elves attack him at +1).

If you defeat him, you can continue to the next room by going to §15 to find out what these creatures are protecting.

§15.

Something dark hovers in the large hall you have entered. This is probably the source of all the problems that have plagued the mine: at the center of the colonnade leading to a dark stone throne, a blinding light comes from a ritual circle. Flashes of light shoot out against the walls. You take cover behind a column to avoid being hit.

You must break the seals in the ritual circle. Each character who tries to do so must roll 1d6. Rogues add +½L to the roll; elves, halflings, witch-hunters and swashbucklers add +L. On a roll of 1-4 you are hit by a ray and must take cover behind a pillar, on a 5-6 you succeed in destroying the arcane symbol. If you get 5 successes (even if not consecutive) go to §36, if a character is hit 3 times (even if not consecutive), go to §37. You can remove one hit on a character using a Blessing.

§16.

The room is empty, except for a small pedestal, covered with a thin purple cloth, on which lays a bright green gemstone.
You may take the gem (worth 35 GP) and then return to §36 to choose another route.

§17.

As you step into the room, you realize you have inadvertently activated a mechanism. A large burst of flame coming from the wall in front of you is about to hit you.

You have activated a trap. Roll d6 for each character in the party. On a roll of 1-2, the character loses 1 Life and if the character carries any scrolls, they are destroyed. On a 3 – 6, the character dodges the trap. Rogues and halflings add +1 to this roll.

The room is empty. You may Search it. On a result of 1, roll on the Wandering Monsters of the Halls of Thoral Table to determine who attacks you. On a 2-4, the room is indeed empty. On a 5-6, you find 1 Sleep scroll and a scarlet gem worth 50 gp.

Then return to §36 to choose another route.

§18.

You descend a large staircase, paying attention to every single step not to slip. You have arrived in the mines of the Peak of Mists. However, the entrance collapsed, and going further into it could be as dangerous as useless. You turn around and continue on your way back to the village of Ranth.

Retrace the rooms and corridors of the Halls of Thoral to return to the village and complete your mission. If you manage to leave the Halls of Thoral, go to the Epilogue section.

§19.

If there is a dwarf or elf in the party, add +1 to the Search result. On a result of 1, roll on the Wandering Monsters of the Halls of Thoral Table to determine who attacks you. On a 2-4, the room is indeed empty (go back to §1 to choose another path). On a 5-6, go to §20 instead.

§20.

At the side you find something written in D'harris (dwarvish language). You inadvertently move a stone in the wall. A mechanism opens a portion of the wall into a dark passage. An icy wind blows from the passage. You may venture inside or retrace your steps.

To descend into the tunnel, go to §9; return to §1 to choose another route.

§21.

You are about to bend down to pick up the items, when suddenly you feel something wet like snail slime dripping on your head. You look up and see a large, gaping mouth full of

sharp spines and fleshy tentacles descending on you.

A monstrous Worm of the Depths attacks you by surprise.

Worm of the Depths, L3 Weird Monster, 4 Life points, Treasure +1, Never tests Morale. Each turn the worm attacks, roll 1d6. On a 1 – 4, the worm catches in its tentacles the party member in the corresponding number of the marching order and swallows the character, on a roll of 5 the worm regurgitates all the swallowed comrades submerging them in an acid fluid that causes the loss of 1 Life point (if before making this roll all the members of the party have been swallowed, you automatically get a roll of 5), while on a roll of 6 it normally attacks a party members).

If you defeat the worm, all swallowed characters are now free and you can collect the long sword and the shield (they are ordinary pieces of equipment), then return to §3 to choose another path.

§22.

If there is an elf or cleric in the party, add +1 to the Search. With a 1-2, go

to §26, with a 3-5 you don't find anything in the corpse, but the nauseating smell causes the first character in marching order to lose 1 Life, with a result of 6 you find 1 Clue (when you find 3 Clues, go to §32).

Then go back to §8 to choose another route.

§23.

The jaws tear at your neck. Hot blood spills copiously from the wound as you see the creature's eyes shining with glee for leading you into its trap.

Roll 1d6 to determine which of your characters is the victim of the attack. On a roll of 1 – 4, the character attacked is the one in the corresponding marching order. If the result is 5-6, you choose who is attacked. The attacked character loses 1 Life and cannot take part in the fight.

Goblin of the Burrow, L3 Minion, No Treasure. The goblin does not move and will not attack your characters. On each of his turns, the character bitten will lose 1 Life. If you kill him with a melee attack, you will cause the loss of 1 additional Life to the bitten companion.

If you kill the goblin with a ranged attack, the victim is freed without further losses.

At the end of the encounter, return to section 8 to continue your mission.

§24.

You push the door and discover it's locked. You observe the mechanism. It shouldn't be complicated to trigger it.

The door has a L3 lock and L 3 strength. If you want to and manage to break in, you may go to §4, otherwise go back to §3 to choose another route.

§25.

You witnessed a long-forgotten ritual of necromancy. The only passage you were able to decipher had the words "Recall" and "Assumed". This information may be useful to share with Elda Shavin, back in town.

Your party gets 1 additional XP roll, however the effort causes the cleric to lose half his/her Life points, rounded down. If you are at 1 Life point you do not lose any Life points but you will have a -1 penalty on the next roll of any type. Return to the paragraph you were in before you found the third Clue.

§26.

Looking more closely at the wound, you see that the goblin's tissues near the deep cut are still slimy and secreting a dark fluid. Something dark has abandoned this creature at the edge of limbo, one step away from eternal sleep. Your astonishment betrays your attention, however, when you notice the little creature lash out at you with unnatural vigor and its mouth wide open, ready to tear at your throat.

If the first character in the marching order is a rogue, roll 1d6 and add +L to the roll. Otherwise roll 1d6 at -1. On a 3+, you succeed the Save against this danger. You get rid of the creature, knocking it to the ground and avoiding its fatal attack (return to §8 to continue your mission). Otherwise go to §23.

§27.

You lean out a little from the edge, pressing your back against the stone wall just enough to allow you to look over. A few meters further on, a door separates you from the voices you hear, but from the shadows you see moving through the wooden beams, you realize that there are more than two people inside.

To enter the room, go to §6,

otherwise go back to §3 and choose another route.

§28.

You take the root out of the bottle and bring it to your mouth. As you chew it, you don't feel any particular flavor at first, but after a few seconds a bitter taste comes down your throat.

Roll 1d6. If the character is a barbarian or halfling or druid, add +3. On a 1, the character is intoxicated (Save vs. L2 poison or lose 1 Life). On a 2-4, nothing happens. On a 5-6, the character heals 1 Life.

Return to the previous paragraph to resume your mission.

§29.

The impact is tremendous, and the splinters pierce the throats and stomachs of two orcs who had their backs to the door. The other survivors widen their eyes and grab their short spears to fight you.

You find yourself in combat with 5 Orcs.

Orcs, L4 Minions, standard Treasure, Never tests Morale. Elves attack them at +1. Orcs are afraid of magic: roll Morale whenever any of them are killed by a spell; if a spell causes their numbers to fall below half, roll at -1. They never have any magic items in their loot: if you get a scroll, treat it as d6xd6 gp instead).

If you defeat them, you can either head to the next door (go to §31), or go back to §3 and choose another path.

§30.

You open the door and find orcs intent on barricading a door on the opposite side of the room. They are using large rocks. One notices your presence and warns his companions, who are gambling at a table. They all watch you, ready to snap at any moment, trying to understand your intentions.

There are 7 Orcs in the room.

Orcs, L4 Minions, Standard Treasure. Elves attack them at +1. Orcs are afraid of magic and must make a Morale roll whenever any of them are killed by a spell; if a spell causes their numbers to fall below half, roll at -1. They never have any magic items in their loot: should you

get a scroll, consider it to be d6xd6 gp instead.

Reactions (d6): 1-4) Bribe (10 gp each), 5-6) fights to the death).

If you survive or avoid this combat, you are forced to go back to §3 and choose another path, as the door in front of you is blocked.

§31.

You defeat the orcs and realize that they were blocking the doorway to another room with heavy boulders. You try to move the rocks, but they are too heavy to be removed quickly. You must retrace your steps and choose another route.

Go back to §3 and choose another route.

§32.

Your party has discovered 1 Secret and immediately gets 1 XP roll.

Inside the Halls, the air becomes more and more poisonous. Breathing causes a pain in your temples and leaves you dizzy. Distorted images appear in your mind: you feel as if you walk through the halls in someone else's bodies, until you reach a large hall with plenty columns. At the end of the hall, at

the foot of a statue, stands a dark stone throne. You realize you are performing a sacrifice within a ritual circle, from which a blinding light emanates. You snap back to reality.

If there's a cleric in your party, the cleric can try to decipher the vision. To do so, go to §25, otherwise go back to the paragraph where you were before finding the third Clue.

§33.

The elf notices some holes in the walls. What appeared to be dampness, to the elf's keen eyes is revealed to be a slimy, gelatinous substance. Stopping to look carefully, you notice some fresh ground falling from the hole in the ceiling, not far from the sword and shield.

If you wish to approach the objects anyway, go to §21, otherwise go back to §3 and choose another route.

§34.

Once the goblins have been defeated, you try to open the door. No matter how hard you try, you realize that something keeps it locked from the opposite side.

Go back to §10 and choose another route.

§35.

The thick wooden door in front of you is barred on the opposite side. You can't see any locks or other ways to open it, but on the other side you can hear the high-pitched, annoying shrieks of goblins and a deeper, more powerful voice that occasionally chuckles with amusement. The only way to find out what lies beyond seems to be to resort to brute force or powerful spells.

The door has a strength of L3. If you manage to break through it, go to §14, or you may go back to §11 and choose another route.

§36.

The light diminishes in intensity until, as you remove the last seal, the room plunges back into darkness. You lean out of the columns again, but are forced to take cover again when a sharp burst of energy erupts from where the ritual circle was before. You are miraculously still alive, unaware of what that last act might have meant. On both sides of the throne, there are two closed doors.

You may also return to the village to tell the burgomaster about your findings.

Your party immediately gets 1 XP roll. From now on, you must refer to the additional note in the Wandering Monsters table of the Halls of Thoral when you encounter Wandering Monsters.

If you want to find out what is behind the doors on either side of the throne, you can try to break in or open them. Both have a L4 lock and a L3 strength. If you break in the left door, go to §16. If you open the right door, go to §17. If in your party there are at least 2 characters belonging to the following classes (barbarian, warrior or dwarf), you may go to §38.

Otherwise, you can retrace your steps to warn the burgomaster Elda Shavin (in this case, if you manage to leave the Halls of Thoral, go to the Epilogue).

§37.

You have to bend down to avoid being hit by a ray as you try to break the magical connection that keeps the ritual alive, but as you get up you are hit by a new burst of energy. You are thrown violently against one of the columns, close to your fellow adventurers. You are just in time to reach out a hand in their direction, with a stifled cry as your breath begins to run out of your lungs. Your companions look on in horror seeing your hand reduced to a pile of dry skin and bones. Suddenly you have a burning

desire to kill them all and defend the ritual circle behind you.

Your companion is dead and transformed into a Skeleton that will immediately attack your party.

Skeleton, L3 Undead Minion, No Treasure, Never tests Morale. Clerics attack the skeleton at +L. Blunt weapons have +1 against skeletons, arrows have -1.

If you fail to defeat the Skeleton in 1 turn, a character of your choice is hit by a ray (from now on consider that the same fate just read to any character hit at least 3 times by a ray from the circle).
You can go back to §15 to interrupt this curse.

§**38**.

Checking the room, you feel a draft of cold air coming from a gap between the statue and the wall. With great effort, two powerful members of the party manage to move the stonework just enough to allow you to pass through the opening.

You may explore the corridor by going to paragraph §18, or retrace your steps to warn the burgomaster Elda Shavin.

Epilogue

When you return to the village, you are greeted with joy by the inhabitants. You have warded off the curse that would have plagued their lands and homes. You retire to a building not far from the main square.
One day later, the burgomaster organizes a great feast, with music and boar stew, to celebrate your success
.
You have successfully completed the adventure! Your party gets 1 XP roll.

Wandering Monsters of the Halls of Thoral Table (d6)

If you have reached §36 all monsters in this Table are also considered Undead and Skeletons in addition to their other traits. Clerics attack them at +L. Blunt weapons have +1 and arrows have -1 when attacking them.

1	**3d6 Pestilential Rats,** L1 Vermin, No Treasure. All characters wounded by the rats have a 1 in 6 chance of losing 1 Life due to the infection and get a -1 to the Attack rolls for the duration of the fight.
2	**d6 Giant Centipedes,** L3 Vermin, No Treasure. All characters wounded must Save vs. L2 poison or lose 1 additional Life.
3	**d6+2 Bats,** L2 Vermin, No Treasure. The Fireball spell attacks them at +2. The party's lantern bearer is not attacked by bats.
4	**d6+3 Night Goblins,** L3 Minions, Treasure -1, Never tests Morale. Dwarves attack them at +1. At the start of each of their turns, roll 1d6. On a 1-5, nothing happens. On a 6, they grab and extinguish your lantern (you cannot relight it until you defeat them).
5	**d6+1 Orcs,** L4 Minions, Standard Treasure. Elves attack them at +1. Orcs are afraid of magic and must make a Morale roll whenever any of them are killed by a spell; if a spell causes their numbers to be halved, roll Morale at -1. They never have any magic items in their loot. If you do get one, treat it as d6xd6 gp instead.
6	**2d6 Thoral Spiders,** L3 Vermin, Treasure -1. All characters wounded by the spiders must Save vs. L3 poison or lose another 1 Life. Blunt Weapons attack them at +1.

25

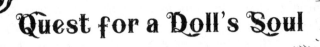

Quest for a Doll's Soul

An adventure for L1 characters

by Frederic Huot and Andrea Sfiligoi

The kukla was originally written by Anna Pashchenko. It was introduced as a playable character class in the Delvers and Wanderers supplement. Owning that book is NOT required to play this adventure, but will give you a better insight into the abilities and background of a Kukla.

Introduction

The Baron's manor is still under alert. It's been three days now since the Orcs assaulted it. The warband has been dealt with, but the Baron is still restless. The Orcs' night raid made a single casualty: Rose, the family's Kukla. Rose had been in the family for generations, caring for the children. The Baron himself had played days on end with the Kukla, as had his father. During the raid the Orcs had gotten close to the children's room. Rose fought them off fiercely. In the end, the Orcs retreated but leaving Rose's body in pieces.

Rose

Rose is a Kukla, a living doll created by a wizard. Kuklas have long prehensile hair and a talent for interacting with children.

Rose had been part of the family for several generations. Her task was always the same: through play, protect and educate the children of the barony. After her tragic demise, the Baron went to a temple to attempt to bring her back, but the ritual failed.

"Rose is unable to reach us. As far as we know, it seems that the Netherworld has taken her. She is now one of the lost souls of the Netherworld."

The Baron was unable to accept this. Had she been in peace, he would grieve her... but this fate was just too cruel.

He contacted a wizard. The wizard told him: "There's a way". He said he could open a portal. A small party of skilled adventurers could enter the Netherworld, restore her soul and bring her back. The wizard would be able to keep the portal open for 12 hours only. He explained the mission as follows:

"There you will find the Kukla and also part of her soul. Those shattered pieces will take the form of Haunts. Solve those haunts to gather the pieces of the soul. Find the Kukla and restore her sanity. You will be threatened by her fears and dark thoughts made manifest."

How to play this adventure

The party is sent through a portal to a part of the Netherworld where Rose has been located. You will explore the place using the tiles in this adventure. You have 2 choices to complete this mission: Either locate the kukla and put her to rest or match the correct special event with the correct haunt to gather the soul pieces in the form of teardrop gems. Bring those gems to the kukla to restore her soul.

The adventure has a time limit of 12 hours that corresponds to the exploration of 72 tiles. If the mission is not

completed by this time, the party will snap back to Norindaal and the mission will be considered a failure.

If you bring back the kukla's soul, the Baron will pay the party 100+ Tier x 100 gp.

Content Warning

This adventure hints at different forms of violence against children. They are not described in detail nor made light of. If this kind of content makes you uncomfortable, do not play this adventure.

Character levels

This adventure uses the HCL (highest character level) system. Meaning that the difficulty of the game will scale with your characters. Characters of any level can play. Level of difficulty of foes and Saves will be calculated using the highest character level in the party. For example, if the highest level in the party is 3, a HCL+3 monster will be Level 6.

Netherworld Tiles

Thorny Briar: This vegetation can be cut to create an opening using a slashing hand weapon or a slashing two-handed weapon. It takes 10 minutes (and 1 roll for wandering monsters) to cut 1 square's equivalent of thorny briars.

Stone: Impassable.

Shack: There is no shelter here. If you decide to explore it, roll a d6 on the following Table:

1	Dungeon: Draw a 5 room dungeon using the standard 4AD tiles. The 5th tile explored should always be a room (reroll if you roll a corridor) and Rose is always found there.
2-4	Roll on the Haunt table. If all haunts have been resolved, count this as a roll of 1.
5-6	Special event: If all special events have been resolved, consider this a Haunt (result 2-4, above). Count it as a Dungeon (result 1, above) if all haunts have been resolved.

No Supervision: there is no Boss. When asked to roll a boss monster, roll d6 on the following Table instead:

1-2	Vermin encounter
3-4	Minion Encounter
5-6	Weird Monster Encounter

Haunts

Haunts are special events that are not real. They are the product of illusion, phantasm and warped perception. Each of them is part of the soul of the Lost Kukla.

Vermin Table (d6)

1	**2d6 Aspects of Darkness**, HCL demons, no treasure. On defense, roll 2 dice and take the lesser value. A Lantern can be used as a weapon against them, with a net +3 to attack rolls, but on a roll of 1 the lantern breaks. *Reactions: 1-3 Prowl: they will follow the party until the next wandering monsters roll and then attack together with any wandering monsters encountered. Multiple encounters of aspects of darkness band together for morale purposes. 4-6 attack.*
2	**1d6 Aspects of Mockery**, HCL+1 demons, no treasure. Ignore all bonuses to defense rolls. Characters cannot run away or escape from this fight. *Reactions: Always Bribe: one character must do something humiliating. The mocking aspects will leave but their numbers are added to the next aspects of mockery Vermin encountered. The humiliated character will be at -1 on all XP rolls until the end of the adventure.*
3	**1d6+1 Aspects of Egotism**, HCL demons, no treasure. When a character fails a defense roll, that character does not lose 1 life but all other characters in the party do instead. *Reaction: Always Bribe (a character must accept exploring the next tile alone. If the party refuses: fight).*
4	**1d6+2 Aspects of Fear**, HCL demons, no treasure. When a character fails a defense check, in addition to losing 1 life, the character must protect his/her own life: drink a healing potion, use bandages, use a healing ability, etc. This is done immediately and does not count as the character's next action. *Reaction: Offer the party to go back to the last tile explored. If the party refuses: fight.*
5	**2d6 Aspects of Loathing**, HCL demons, no treasure. When a character fails a defense roll, in addition to taking damage the character cannot use any ability, spells or use items on next turn. Can only attack. *Reaction: Always fight.*
6	**1d6+4 Aspects of Anger**, HCL demons, no treasure. On an Attack roll of 1, the character throws his/her weapon away and must fight bare-handedly at -2. The thrown weapon can be recovered after the fight. *Reaction: always fight to the death.*

	Minion Table (d6)
1	**2d6 Aspects of Bullying**, HCL+2 demons, normal treasure, morale -2. Their attacks inflict 2 damage. *Reaction: Always Bribe (5 gp each).*
2	**2d6 Aspects of Harassment**, HCL+1 demons, 2 treasure rolls at -2. Every turn, 1 additional Aspect of Harassment joins the fight, until all are destroyed. *Reaction: Always fight to the death.*
3	**1d6+4 Aspects of Overprotection**, HCL+2 demons, no treasure, morale +4. *Reaction: They reveal the content of the next tile (roll it before entering the tile) but no treasure or XP roll may be gained by visiting that tile.*
4	**2d6 Aspects of Sadness**, HCL demons, normal treasure, morale +1. Every turn until they are destroyed, they gain 1 L. *Reaction: Offer the party to return to the entrance tile or fight.*
5	**2d6 Aspects of Starvation**, HCL+1 demons, normal treasure. When a starving aspect attacks a character, it will keep attacking the same character every turn. The starving aspect only changes target when the character is dead. *Reaction: Always Bribe (1d6 food for the whole group).*
6	**1d6+2 Aspects of Violence**, HCL+1 demons, 2 attacks, 1 treasure, morale -1. *Reaction: always fight*

Weird Monsters Table (d6)

1	**Aspect of Manipulation**, HCL+3 demon, HCL+1 life, 1 treasure, morale -1. When the Aspect of Manipulation loses 1 life from a character's actions, that character also loses 1 life. *Reaction: The aspect will not attack if the characters agree to go back to the previous tile. The demon will stay on its current tile.*
2	**Aspect of Neglect**, HCL+3 demon, 8 life, 1 treasure, morale +2. The Aspect of Neglect will not attack any character. Instead, one random character automatically loses 1 Life every turn, until the demon is defeated. *Reaction: always fight.*
3	**Aspect of Shame**, HCL+2 demon, 5 life, 2 treasure. The aspect of Shame attacks all characters once per turn. *Reactions (d6): 1-4 Flee, 5-6 fight.*
4	**Aspect of Abandonment**, HCL+4 demon, 6 life, 2 treasure. If it is alive at the beginning of turn 3, the Aspect will flee. If it flees this way, you do not get its treasure and XP roll. *Reactions (d6): 1-2 flee 3-6 fight.*
5	**Aspect of Despair**, HCL+2 demon, 4 life, 1 treasure, morale +2. On all Attack and Defense rolls against this Aspect, roll 2 dice and take the lower. *Reaction: It will not fight if you agree to spend 1 hour with him. Do not roll for wandering monster but lose 1 hour (of the 12 total before the portal closes).*
6	**Aspect of Abuse**, HCL+2 demon, 4 life, 1 treasure, morale -2. Life lost from its attacks can be healed ONLY by natural means (bandages and time) or with a Blessing spell that will heal 1d6+ Caster's L. *Reaction: The aspect will offer 1 treasure. If you accept, you gain the treasure but your next encounter with vermin, minion or weird monster will automatically be with an Aspect of Abuse with +2 L.*

Treasure Table (d6)	
1	2d6 gp
2	4d6 gp
3	Gem worth 2d6x5 gp
4	Gem worth 4d6x5 gp
5	Roll on the Magic item Table
6	Choose: roll on the Magic Item Table at +1 or find 1 Soul Cube (from *Four Against the Netherworld*).

Magic Item Table (d6)	
1	**Demonic Serrated Knife**: This knife deals Tier+1 damage. On an Attack roll of 1, the blade snaps and must be discarded. Resale value: 300 gp.
2	**Animated Doll**: This small wooden doll will obey any command. It has one Life and can fight with no Attack and Defense bonuses. It can carry up to 20 gp and 2 small items like scrolls, potions or knives. Resale value: 200 gp.
3	**Clockwork Parrot**: This small artificial bird can carry small items (lantern, dagger, scroll, potion, or messages). It cannot attack. It can travel long distances to deliver what it is carrying. Resale value: 200 gp.
4	**Ring of Caring**: This ring can be worn only by a cleric. It allows the cleric to use an extra Healing or Blessing per adventure. Resale value: 250 gp. Additional Rings of Caring are NOT cumulative.
5	**Glasses of the Watchmaker**: These spectacles give the wearer +1 to lockpicking and disarming traps rolls. They can be worn only by those who can perform those rolls. Resale value: 200 gp.
6	**Comb of Good Luck**: When used to comb the owner's hair before an adventure, it gives its owner the equivalent of 1 Luck point (like the halfling ability of the same name). May not be used by characters without hair, such as lizardmen and kobolds. Resale value: 200 gp.

Special Events Table (d6)

1	You find an old, broken wooden toy horse. It seems to have been painted white and green but the paint is faded and dirty. The wood is cracked. You can take it. If you do so, ignore this Special Event if you roll it again.
2	You find 2 small wooden toy knight figures. They have been left in the mud too long with no one to care for them. You can take them. If you do so, ignore this Special Event if you roll it again.
3	You find some puppets on the ground. Some are torn apart and look like bits of ragged clothes in the mud. You can take them. If you do, ignore this Special Event if you roll it again.
4	You find a small toy bow and a few bent arrows, too light to count as weapons. The bowstring is broken. You can take them. If you do so, ignore this Special Event if you roll it again.
5	You find a small brass flute, covered in mud. If you take it, ignore this Special Event if you roll it again.
6	You find a broken clay pot with a spoon. You may take it if you want. If you take it, ignore this Special Event if you roll it again.

Haunts Table (d6)

1	A little girl is playing with a black and red wooden horse. She says: "Hello, you like my new horse? His name is Gloom. I miss my old horse. Her name was Joy and she was white as the sun and green as the forest. She was the best. I lost her." If you have the wooden horse, you can give it to the girl. The haunt will vanish and you will be left with a teardrop gem. If you take it, this haunt will not appear again.
2	A little boy is playing with a small castle made of sticks. He is adding sticks in a circle around the castle. "This is my castle. There are no more knights to defend it so I am putting stakes to keep everyone away." If you have the wooden Knight figures you can give them to the boy. The haunt will vanish and you will be left with a teardrop gem. If you take it, this haunt will not appear again.
3	A little girl is talking to the air. "Wanna play with us? You can't see my friends, only I can. I miss my puppets, I used to make plays and my friends would come and see them. Now I lost them, and no one is interested in a play you cannot see or hear." If you have the puppets, you can give them to the girl. The haunt will vanish and you will be left with a teardrop gem. If you take it, this haunt will not appear again.
4	You see a little boy throwing small rocks at a wooden cup. "Hi, wanna play? The rules are simple: when you throw a rock inside the cup you can play again, if you miss it's the other's turn. When we have played 3 times each we count how many rocks each of us have. I know it's a bit boring. I used to have a bow, I was good with it. I wanted to become one of the King's archers. Now it is gone, I guess I'll never be anything." If you have the toy bow, you can give it to the boy. The haunt will vanish and you will be left with a teardrop gem. If you take it, this haunt will not appear again.
5	You see a little girl digging a hole in the ground with a stick. "Wanna help me? I'm digging here. Not sure why, I guess I am bored. I used to never be bored. I had a brass flute that I would play. I would play a new melody every day. It was awesome. I lost it. So I cannot play it anymore." If you have the brass flute, you can give it to the girl. The haunt will vanish and you will be left with a teardrop gem. If you take it, this haunt will not appear again.
6	A little boy is making a small bundle of briars. He is trying to hug it some way or another. "My nanny used to make me jam with the strawberries we gathered in the forest. She would give it to me with a spoon, no bread. She always gave me a huge hug afterward. After a while, every time I ate the jam I would remember her hug. I miss the hug more than the jam. I made this. If I hug it hard enough maybe I will remember my nanny again?" If you have the broken clay pot, you can give it to the boy. The haunt will vanish and you will be left with a teardrop gem. If you take it, this haunt will not appear again.

Rose, the lost Kukla

Turn here when you encounter the Lost Kukla.

As you advance through the darkness, you notice a lot of Thorny Briar around you covering the walls. You arrive to an open chamber. A small doll sits in a corner. The Thorny Briars are coming out of her head. They are actually the extension of what used to be Rose's hair. Rose is staring at you. Her eyes are black and look as if not really seeing. What look like black tears stains her face and her tattered robe.

The thorny briars are shaking. Rose is pulled up by the briars.

If you have 6 teardrop gems, go to Saved. If not, fight Rose as a final boss.

Rose the lost Kukla, HCL+5 Artificial Weird Monster, HCL+4 life, 2 attacks, 1 treasure +2. Every turn, Rose creates little automaton dolls while the thorny briars attack. Add 1 automaton doll at the beginning of every turn.

Automaton Doll: HCL artificial minion, 1 life, 1 attack, no treasure.

If you defeat her, go to Put to Rest.

Put to Rest

There was no saving her, not with the means at your disposal. You did the best thing and put the poor soul to rest. Now the family will be able to grieve. When you return to the portal, you notice the thorny briars have turned white and are crumbling away.

Saved

You extend the 6 teardrop gems. They glow green. As if in answer to them, Rose's eyes light up with a green reflection for the briefest of moments. Suddenly, the doll seems to find a renewed vigor. The Kukla pulls away from the briars. She manages to reach your hand and grab the green gems. Holding them to her chest with one hand and defending against the briar with the other. Her black long hair pulls away from the briars. As more hair is freed, leaving the briars hollow and lifeless, she is more and more able to defend herself. After moments, all the briars turn white. Some crumble away.

Rose seems to have found joy again.

"I miss the kids. Let's go see them, there is nothing else here."

Back at the Baron's Manor, you receive a reward of 100 + Tier x 100 gp.

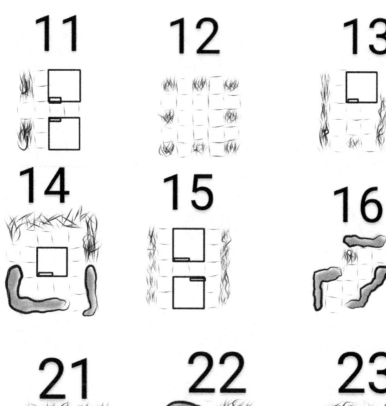

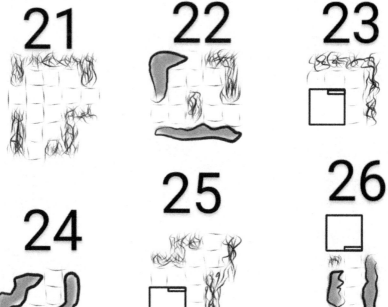

31

32

33

34

35

36

41
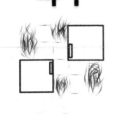

42

43

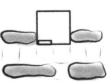

44

45

46

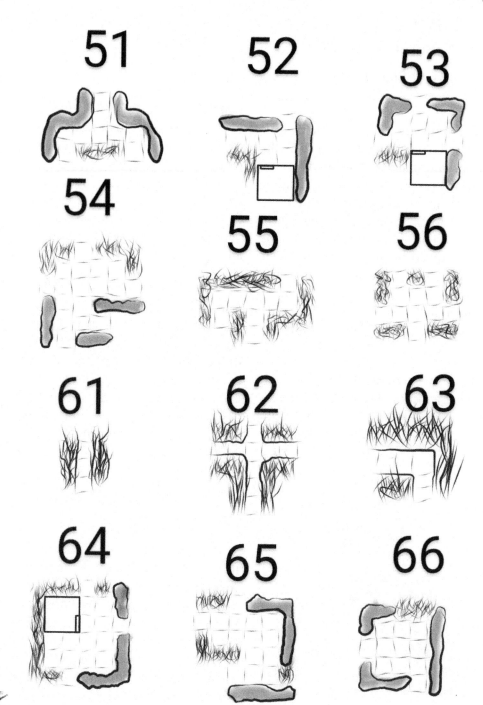

4AD Houserule: Holy Symbols Expanded

By William C. Pfaff

Upon attaining L7 (or higher) and in place of selecting an Expert Skill, clerics can instead elect to receive a specially prepared magic holy symbol from their church as a reward for their service to the cause. This weapon is protected by divine forces and cannot be destroyed by normal means. Iron Eaters cannot affect it and gremlins cannot steal it. It cannot be sundered and a monster cannot make the cleric lose or drop the holy symbol in combat.

Each holy symbol acts as a weapon and has additional powers as noted. A cleric receives the holy symbol from the domain that best matches their

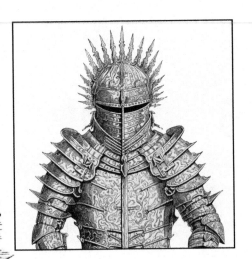

personal deity. The cleric can receive this boon only once, thus they cannot expend two expert skills to gain two holy symbols.

Domains of Sun and Healing

This holy symbol manifests as a +1 magical mace (hand, crushing weapon) with a gleaming gold sunburst design topping it. The top glows when wielded and provides light equal to a lantern. Anytime the owner of this uses the healing power it restores +1 additional life.

Domains of Law of Oaths

This holy symbol manifests as a +1 magical broadsword (hand, slashing weapon) with various writs and laws of the order painstakingly carved into the handle. The blade glows when wielded and provides light equal to a lantern. Anytime the owner rolls a 1 on an attack roll against a creature with the word "Chaos" in its name, they may re-roll the attack.

Domains of Storms and Lightning

This holy symbol manifests as a +1 magical cudgel (hand, crushing weapon) with a swirling storm nebulous that appears to be constantly roiling at the top. The cudgel glows when wielded and provides light equal to a lantern. Once per adventure the owner may cast lightning bolt as if they were a wizard of equal level.

Domains of Death and the Underworld

This holy symbol manifests as a +1 magical mace (hand, crushing weapon) with a dark violet skull motif atop it. The skull constantly whispers dark secrets to its owner (once per adventure the owner of this symbol can gain a clue). The owner of this weapon can change undead vermin or minion's reaction to "peaceful" once per adventure.

Domains of War and Glory

This holy symbol manifests as a +1 magical hammer (hand, crushing weapon) with a perpetually blood red tinge to the metal. The hammer provides a +1 bonus to Defense, as it revels in its owner being in the thick of battle. The hammer has a downside in that it encourages battle. Any enemy rolling the "fight reaction" fights to the death instead.

Domains of Music and Beauty

This holy symbol manifests as a +1 magical rapier (hand, slashing weapon) with a hollow handle with multiple holes. The owner can allow the wind to pass through it or they can blow lightly across the holes to create a soothing melody. Once per day this melody can be played for a single character, removing 1 point of Madness. This holy symbol will release a warning whistle sound to allow those in the back ranks to know of an attack from wandering monsters. This gives them the chance to use their shield as part of their first Defense roll.

Domain of Fertility

This holy symbol manifests as a +1 magical mace (hand, crushing weapon). Carved bodies intertwined in the throes of ecstasy decorate the handle. The owner of this symbol adds +1 to both wooing and giving rolls.

New Weird Monster:

Zvuk, the Trumpeteer

By Anna Pashchenko and Andrea Sfiligoi

HCL+4 weird monster, HCL+6 Life (minimum 8), 3 attacks (1 bite, inflicting Tier damage, and 2 claw strikes, inflicting 1 damage each), Trumpeteer ability, Morale+1, 2 Treasure rolls + Magic Trumpets+ Glass.

A Zvuk is a shapeshifting creature which feeds on human feelings of fear and anxiety. It was generated by extra-dimensional energies in a town under siege, where such feelings were prevalent. Initially it was a unique being, but with time it grew and managed to create "copies" of itself, spreading to other towns.

The creature's main shape is a thin, transparent veil that can cover a whole city block. It can be noticed only by elves and wizards as a grey shadow floating in the sky, or as a translucent yellowish ectoplasm spread over buildings. Noticing it is difficult: you may do so only on a successful Search roll. The creature can lay dormant in this state for years, and then suddenly take its humanoid shape to attack.

This will happen if it is discovered by an adventuring party and feel threatened, or if the Zvuk is feeling hungry.

Its secondary humanoid form has a single large eye and a round mouth full of glass-like shards (that can bite for Tier damage). It has yellowish-green skin and long, flexible arms ending in clawed hands (capable of a damage 1 attack). But its main ability is its brass trumpets protruding from small "mouths" on its skin. These trumpets produce a scary, deafening cacophony that can strike terror into non-heroic characters. The Zvuk will blare its trumpets every turn. All hirelings or other NPCs accompanying the party have a 1 in 6 chance of fleeing the encounter every turn. Ignore this rule if the party includes a lionman or a paladin, or if a spell is cast on the creature creating magic Silence. If the Zvuk is encountered in a dungeon, roll a d6 for all hirelings escaping the combat: on a 1, the hireling is found dead 1 room/area later, with their equipment intact; on a 2-3, the hireling disappears forever, on a 4-6 the hireling is met again d3 rooms/areas/hexes later, still shocked but unharmed.

Heroes hearing the trumpets must Save vs. HCL sound or suffer one of the following effects (chosen by the player):

1) Be temporarily deafened. This makes the character immune to the cacophony for the rest of the encounter, but also makes it impossible for the character to cast spells or gain the advantage of Blessing; Deafness disappears as soon as any form of magical healing is used on the character;

2) Lose TWO memorized spells;

3) Take 2 damage due to internal bleeding and split eardrums;

4) Be at -Tier on all Attacks until the end of the encounter (you may choose this effect only once);

5) Drop all handheld shields and weapons.

6) Cry; this causes the Zvuk to regenerate Tier life points immediately. If you choose this option, keep track of how many points the Zvuk has regenerated, as it may lose them later.

The creature has two Secret Weaknesses. Revealing each of them costs 3 Clues (2 if the party subscribes to the Beast Bulletin from *The Dreadful Dozen* supplement).

Weakness 1: The Zvuk's eye is vulnerable to a mixture of lemon juice, salt, pepper. All these ingredients are automatically available if the party has a halfling or an ogre grubman or any other "cook" character in its ranks. If these characters are not available, assume that the ingredients can be bought for 1 gp in any settlement.

If the mixture is thrown into the Zvuk's eye (this requires 1 Turn but is automatic, i.e., no Attack roll is needed), the Zvuk takes Tier damage and loses the ability to play its trumpets.

Weakness 2: The Zvuk loves the smell of burning things. You may distract it by using a Fireball, or any other fire-based spell or ability (like a fire elf's optic blast) to put something on fire. When you do so, the Zvuk's L will be halved for 3 turns, and it will not play its trumpets while being distracted.

Treasure: In addition to some random treasure that probably belonged to its former victims, the Zvuk's teeth can be fashioned into d6+1 glass knives (cheap masterwork light slashing weapons; resale value 6 gp each; they break and must be discarded on the roll of 1 on any Attack roll).

Its d6+2 trumpets are magical. They have a resale value of 25 gp each. Each trumpet can be used a single time to cause a Morale roll at -2 for any foe that is not an undead or artificial, or to automatically inflict

Tier+1 damage to any crystal creature (against Minor Foes, each point of Damage will destroy 1 creature).

Unfortunately, using the Trumpet also causes 2 damage to the user, and shatters the Trumpet.

Setting Up Camp

An adventure for L1 characters, to be used before the party enters a dungeon.

Written by Frédéric Huot

Introduction

The heroes have traveled quite a distance today. Nothing major has troubled them. They are now ready to set up camp for the night.

It is still a couple of hours before dark. The party will sleep. A single hero will stay awake and keep watch. This region is not very dangerous and major foes are not expected. Minor foes are a possibility. A fire will provide warmth and keep away vermin.

The party has the equivalent of the exploration of 30 tiles to secure the surroundings and gather dry wood for the bonfire. The fastest way is to split the party. Here is how it works:

- Use the map and tiles provided.

- Split the group in 2. Each half of the party will explore the surrounding terrain, forming a circle around the camp and reaching the other side of the road, covering all the marked spots and leaving no unexplored squares between the marked spot and the road.

- The characters also need to gather 40 bundles of dry wood.

- The two halves of the party can begin anywhere on the road and must be back on the road before dark.

If you succeed, your party is going be fully rested for the next adventure.

- Restore all lost life and all uses of abilities.

- Gain +1 to Attack or Defense rolls (your choice for each character) for the duration of the next adventure.

If you fail, the party is unable to secure their campsite. They have to stand watch and are only able to get very little sleep. In this case, the rest is partial and you restore only 1 life and 1 use of an ability.

Minions slain during this adventure count as normal for XP purposes (1 XP per every 10 groups encountered and defeated).

Rules

When crossing already explored tiles, do not roll for wandering monsters.

When asked to roll for weird monsters, roll for vermin instead, but double their numbers. When asked to roll for boss monsters, roll for minions instead, but double their numbers.

Trees can be cut. This requires an axe and 10 minutes to cut the equivalent of 1 square. Cut trees are not dry enough to be used as firewood.

Picking up firewood: A successful Search roll may be used to find 1d3 bundles of dry wood instead of 1 Clue. A special event may grant a variable quantity of firewood.

Special features are rolled as special events.

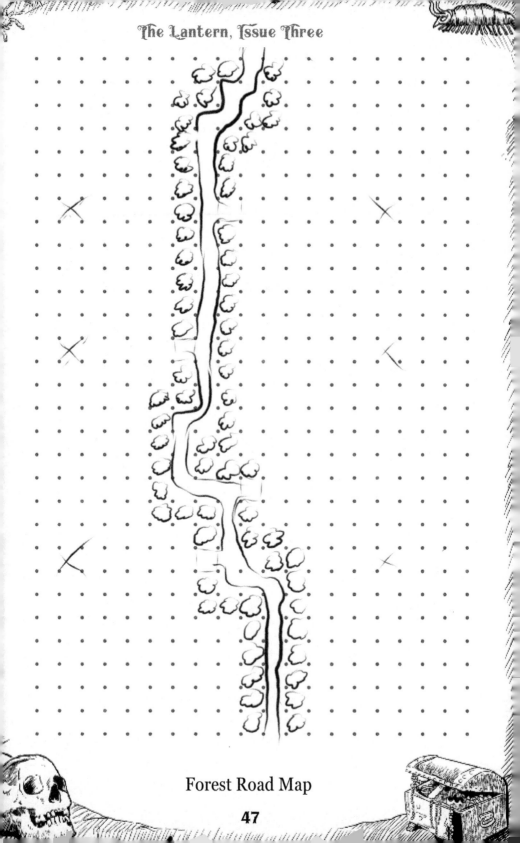

Forest Road Map

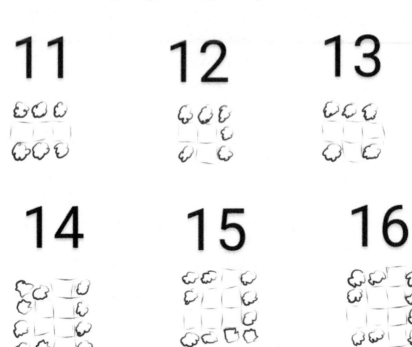

11
12
13
14
15
16

21
22
23
24
25
26

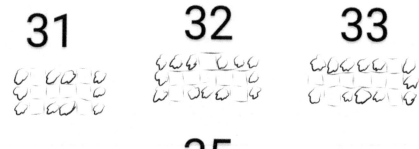

31
32
33

34
35
36

41
42
43

44
45
46

51

52

53

54

55

56

61

62

63

64

65

66

Setting Up Camp Vermin Table (d6)

1	**1d6 hungry muskrats**, L1 animal Vermin, no treasure. Throwing 1 ration at the hungry muskrats ends the combat. *Reaction: Always Bribe (1 ration to bribe the whole group).*
2	**1d6 treetop spiders**, L1 vermin, no treasure. Their bite causes severe itching that prevent casting spells and cleric prayers (Blessing, Healing) for 10 minutes per the number of bites suffered. This includes casting spells from scrolls, but not from magic items like wands, rods, etc. *Reaction: always fight.*
3	**1d6+1 emaciated wolves**, L2 animal vermin, 2 attacks, no treasure, morale -2 *Reaction: always fight*
4	**1d6+1 animated skeleton hands**, L2 undead vermin, no treasure. Always surprise. Bludgeoning weapon hit them at +1. Reaction: always fight to the death.
5	**1d6+2 ghoul squirrels**, L2 undead vermin, no treasure. When bitten by a ghoul squirrel, Save vs. L4 poison or get -2 to all rolls on the next turn. Clerics and all elves add +L, dwarves and halflings add + ½ L. *Reaction: always fight to the death*
6	**1d6+2 forest bat-things**, HCL animal vermin, no treasure, Morale -1. *Reactions (d6): 1- flee, 2-6 fight*

Setting Up Camp Minions Table (d6)

1	**1d6 chicken thieves**, L3 minions, treasure: 1 live chicken each. Each live chicken is worth 5 gp or may be eaten (equivalent to 1 ration). Morale: -1 *Reactions (d6): 1-3 flee, 4-6 Fight*
2	**1d6 goblin house raiders**, L3 minions, treasure: 1d3 pan or pots + 1d3 kitchen knives, worth 1 gp each. *Reaction: always bribe: 1 weapon or armor of any kind.*
3	**1d6 +1 road muggers** L3 minions, treasure: 2d6 gp. Muggers' attacks deal 2 damage. Note this damage separately. If all character in the party fall to 0 life: the party wakes up later, having lost all gp, gems, jewelry (including magic rings and amulets) and 30 minutes but all damage inflicted by the muggers is healed. *Reaction: Always Bribe: 3d6 gp*
4	1d6 +1 Goblin hunters L3 minions, treasure: 2 javelins (light ranged weapon) each. Goblin hunters always attack first unless a character has a ranged weapon drawn. *Reactions (d6): 1-3 Bribe (1d6 Food rations or 1 live chicken), 4-6 fight*
5	1d6 +2 Horse thieves, L3 minions, treasure: 1 horse (resale value 60 gp) *Reactions (d6): 1-2 flee, 3-6 fight*
6	1d6+2 Goblin road raiders L3 attacks: 2, treasure: 3d6 gp. *Reaction: always fight*

Setting Up Camp Traps Table (d6)

1	**Hidden Spike Trap**: L3, a random character loses 1 life.
2	**Hidden Snare**: L3, a random character gets caught. If the party has at least 1 slashing weapon, the party loses 10 minutes cutting the ropes. If the party does not have a slashing weapon, the party loses 30 minutes.
3	**Hidden Net**: all characters save L4. Any character failing the save is caught in a hanging net above the ground. If the character caught has at least 1 light slashing weapon, the party loses 10 minutes. If the party has a hand slashing weapon or a 2 handed slashing weapon, the party loses 30 minutes. If the party has no slashing weapons at all, the party loses 2 hours.
4	**Bear Trap**, L4: A random character loses 1 life and the party loses 10 minutes
5	**Spikefall trap**: all characters in the party save at L4, any hero failing the Save loses 1 life and the party loses 10 minutes.
6	You find a snare with a rabbit caught in it. Gain 1 Food ration.

Setting Up Camp Special Events Table (d6)

1	**Dead tree**: its branches are dry and away from the ground's humidity. Gain d6+1 bundles of dry wood.
2	**Old camp**: You find the traces of an old campsite. There is wood stacked. Some is wet and rotten but those on the top are dry. Gain 1 bundle of dry wood.
3	**Patch of medicinal herbs**: Some medicinal plants are growing here. You can spend 10 minutes gathering 1d6+1 doses. Each dose, when used with bandages, makes bandages heal 2 life points instead of 1.
4	**Deer**: You stumble on a deer or similar animal. If a character has a bow ready, the deer can be killed with an Attack roll against L3. If successful, you gain 1d6+4 Food rations. If the roll fails, the deer flees. A character can only carry a single deer.
5	**Abandoned shack**: This old shack is falling apart. The wood used to build it is dry. The party can spend 10 minutes gathering 1d6+1 bundles of dry wood.
6	**Dungeon entrance**: You have found the entrance of a small dungeon. If you have the time you may explore it. Generate a dungeon using the core book until you encounter 1 major foe (weird monster or boss). At that point, the dungeon ends. Exploring the dungeon is optional and can be played as a separate adventure.

Using Pre-generated Maps

Written by Daniel Casquilho

A key mechanic in *Four Against Darkness* is the random generation of maps. Exploring the unknown with your party, even you do not know what will come next. However, in some game sessions, you may chose to use pre-generated maps. I have at times. I started to use pre-generated maps to reduce the time it takes to run a short dungeon crawl. I began to run small games during my lunch break and found that by eliminating the generation and drawing of the map I could get a lot more done in the 45 minutes that I had. It started as a practical tradeoff for me.

Talking to other players, I found some who do not like their own hand-drawn maps but prefer the look of pre-generated maps. Nicely drawn maps make the game more immersive for them. Pre-generated maps can help set a theme or feel to a dungeon. Want lots of undead? A pre-generated crypt system would work. Want a dwarven mine? There are wonderful maps showing mines out there. Maps can add to the theme of a particular game session when combined with the right monsters.

Looking for maps can be part of the fun of the game as well. There are lots of sources. Start with your existing RPG collection. Any adventure module from other games, game magazines, or even some rule sets have maps in them. I found a lot

of usable maps in places like the old *Dungeon Magazine*. Issue 14, page 9 had a great little 5 room dungeon lair for example. Game modules like *DF20 Voices of the Three* from the *Castles and Crusades* RPG has a great two level dungeon map that I used over a few sessions for a wonderful dungeon crawl. Another example from my collection: *The Lair of Maylock* from the Judges Guild book *Book of Ruins* made for a great weekend long crawl. Other game systems may use different markings on their maps but in the end a map is a map.

complex to be explored by a party searching for missing townsfolk. The map of the local mall can be turned into an elaborate catacomb; a map of the local amusement park can become a haunted town. You can get maps of real places when you visit them or find them on the internet. Famous churches, catacombs, museums, schools, ruins, castles, and various other locations are often just a click away.

Let's not forget that Alexey Aparin sells, on Drivethrucards, official 4AD card decks for generating maps (at the moment of writing, there are three sets available) and Ganesha Games has a Dungeon Atlas, with more coming. This is a collection of 21 pre-drawn dungeons. Each comes with a map of numbered rooms on the left page and a corresponding form on the right page that you fill in as you progress through the maze. You may photocopy or print out the dungeons and reuse them as many times as you want.

Another great source are maps of real places. You can get maps from various sources that can be used as fantasy maps. Travel or science magazines like *National Geographic* often have maps in them. Other maps can come from the locations themselves that you may visit; The Getty Museum, for example, gave my family a map of their grounds that became a great abandoned

If you search the Internet for "tiny dungeon map" or "small dungeon map", many options will open to you, from sites where people offer their maps for free download such as the blog by *Dyson Logos* or *Daniel's Maps* to people like *The Reclusive Cartographer* on Facebook or Instagram. There are also web-based programs that generate maps such as One Page Dungeon (watabou.itch.io/one-page-dungeon). The internet can be a real bounty for maps, often cost nothing or tiny amounts.

Lastly I have also bought or downloaded for free some resources from DriveThruRPG. The site has many different resources ranging from one page items to large books. If you buy, keep an eye out for good deals. I picked up some "one page adventures" that came with an intro, plot ideas, and NPCs/monsters already statted out for another fantasy RPG, and a great map for a very small sum in their summer sale for example.

Once I find a map I like, there are a few things I do to it before I put it in my "for use" stack. I look at the map and mark it up; I number the rooms and corridors so I can track them easy in generating the content as I play, if the separation between rooms or corridors is not clear I use a red pen and make a small red line that shows where one room or corridor ends and the next begins. If a corridor is very long, I break it into two or three sections depending on the layout and length. I have also added doors at times using a red pen to draw door symbols on the map. I also note secret doors that the map may have. Sometimes I turn them into normal doors, treating some as locked doors. I use a house rule, where a party that enters a space with a secret door has a '2 in 6' chance to detect the door. I have used maps where the party didn't notice some secret doors.

Next I look for any special features I may need to house rule or make into an encounter or event. Features like a waterfall, river, chasm, lava pits, or cliff all might require you to think through how you want to incorporate them into your game. If there is a cliff, ropes and climbing Saves might be involved, for example. In some cases you can ignore them but in

other cases it is worth noting them on the map. Sometimes I jot down a Save on the map at those locations. Other times I turn them into their own special encounter, for example a chasm is a great place for a Major Foe encounter. Wear your game master's hat to add fun to a map!

Next I may note what rules would be used in that specific map. If it is an outdoor location, then lanterns may not be needed during the day. If it is a multi-level dungeon location such as the map mentioned above, will the challenge levels go up when you descend a level? Lastly, be clear what Final Boss rule you will use; will you roll as outlined in *Four Against Darkness*, or use a timer, or just say the last room regardless of the number of major foes encountered will be the Final Boss? This is an important decision, because large maps may require more than one session to complete.

I place my marked up maps in a folder and pull them out as needed, ready to go.

Try to use pre-generated maps. I hope your game will be fun and a success for your characters as well as yourself.

Printed in Great Britain
by Amazon